The Secret Life of Mushrooms

Contents

Written by Inbali Iserles

Collins

After the rain

Under a full moon, mushrooms grow in the damp earth. Their round heads bob on the breeze.

Mushrooms are different
to plants. They are
the fruits of a fungus.

In many ways, mushrooms are closer to animals than plants. Plants use sunshine, water and air to make their own food.

Like an animal, a fungus cannot make its own food. It feeds off other things.

An animal swallows its food.

A fungus pulls in food through branching roots.

Friendly fungus?

Mushrooms play a useful role in the cycle of life and death.

Some kinds of fungus are parasites. This one is eating a fly.

Others feed on tree trunks or rotting fruit.

Fungus facts

Scientists have found hundreds of thousands of different sorts of fungus.

Fungal networks

A small mushroom in the grass could be part of a much bigger fungus that grows under the earth.

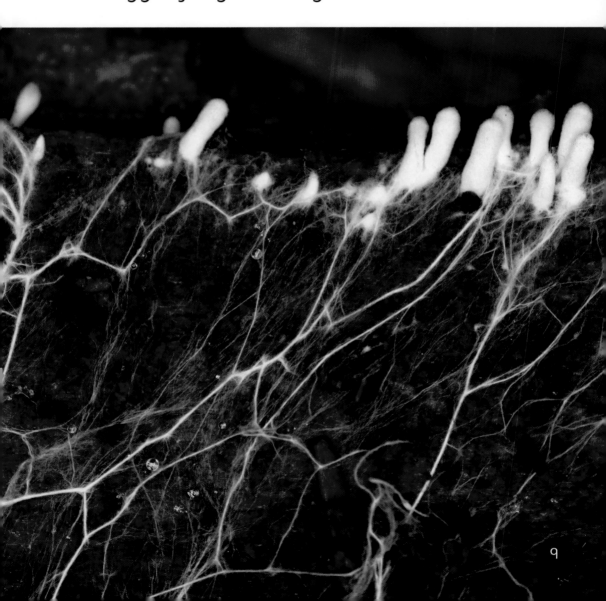

Fungal **networks** link lots of mushrooms together. The mushrooms share food and water.

Fungus facts

The largest living thing in the world is a fungal network. It is bigger than a blue whale!

Where can we find different kinds of fungus?

Everywhere!

Fungus grows on the forest floor, in water, in our bodies and even in the air!

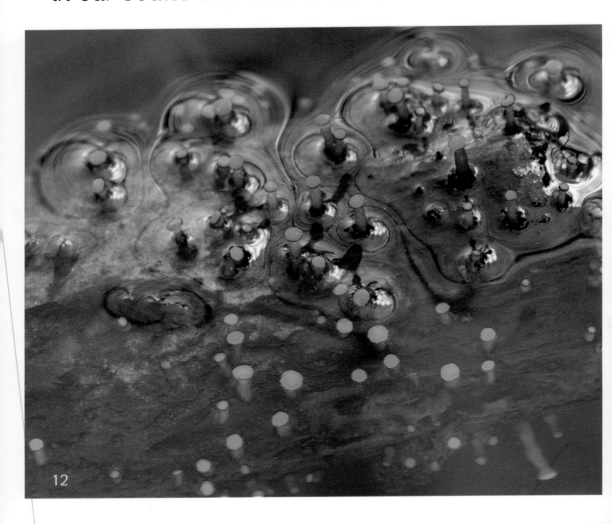

Fungus facts

The smallest fungus can only be seen with a **microscope**.

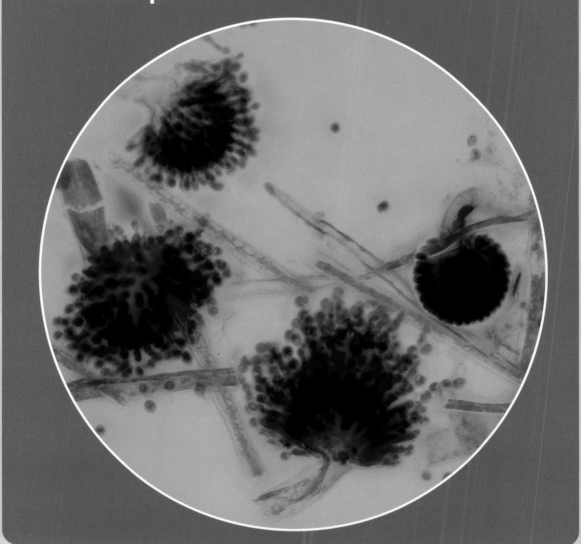

Fungus in science

Some kinds of fungus are used in hospitals and **medical research**.

Fungus facts

A fungus mould called "penicillin" helps to fight disease in humans.

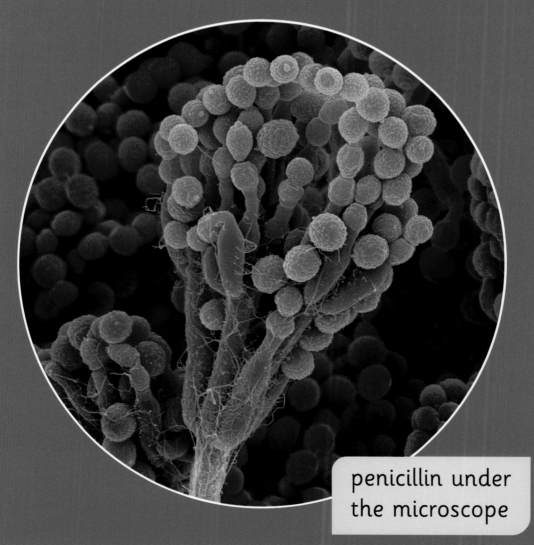

penicillin under the microscope

Beware!

Some mushrooms contain poison. Eating them can cause death. Even touching one could make you ill.

Keep your distance!

17

A lot to learn

Mushrooms have existed on earth longer than most living things. New kinds of fungus are always being discovered!

There is so much to learn about fungus!

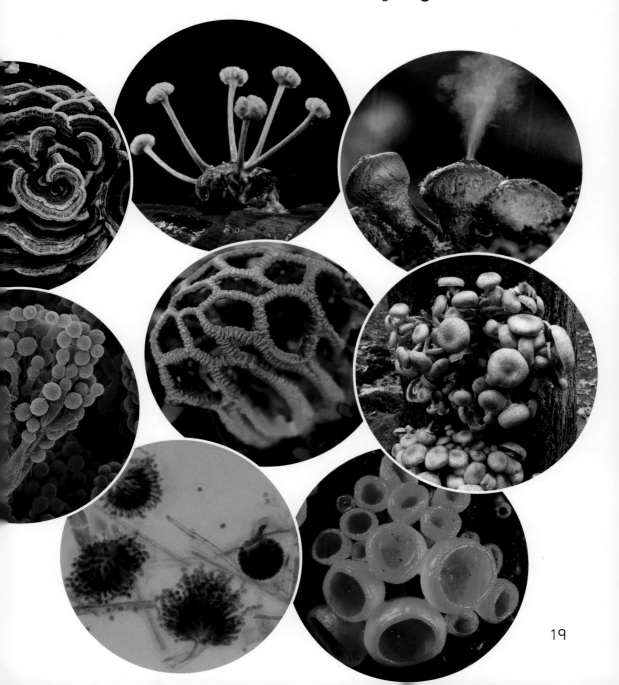

Glossary

medical to do with the treatment of illness

microscope a device that makes tiny objects look bigger

networks a number of things that are linked together

research work that involves studying something

Index

Amazing fungus

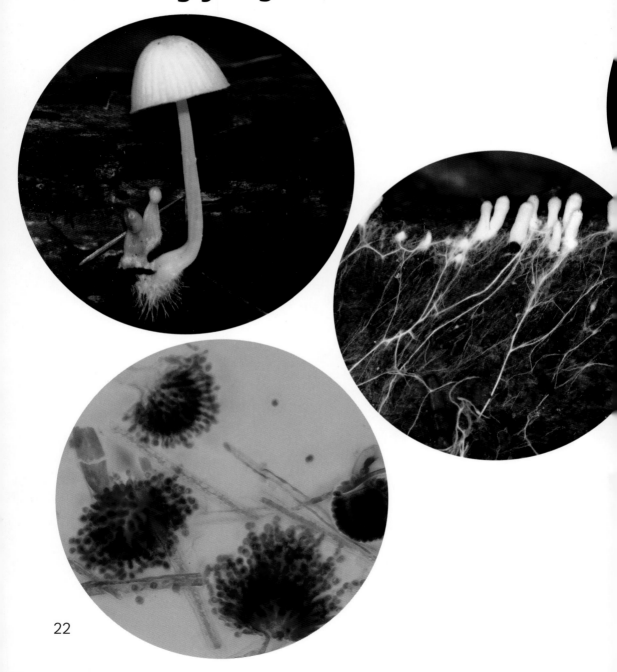

Review: After reading

Use your assessment from hearing the children read to choose any GPCs, words or tricky words that need additional practice.

Read 1: Decoding

- Focus on /or/ sounds in longer words. Ask the children to read the words and identify the letters that make the /or/ sound. Say: Look out for the word that does not contain an /or/ sound. (**world**)

  water (*a*)   **floor** (*oor*)   **world**   **cause** (*au*)   **always** (*al*)

- Point to the following words, challenging the children to blend the sounds in their heads.

  page 2 **earth**   **breeze**   page 5 **swallows**   **branching**   page 17 **careful**

Read 2: Prosody

- Discuss how commas are used to break up sentences. Model reading page 4, then ask:
  - Why is this comma here, in the first sentence? (*It separates **In many ways** from the main part of the sentence.*)
  - Why is this comma here, in the next sentence? (*It is used to separate things in a list.*)
- Ask the children to read the top of page 5, checking they pause at the comma. Discuss how the comma is used to separate the phrase **Like an animal** which keeps the comparison (between an animal and a fungus) going.

Read 3: Comprehension

- Ask the children to describe their experiences of seeing mushrooms in the wild or mushrooms as a type of food.
- Discuss the title. Ask: Do you think mushrooms have a secret life? What bits of a mushroom's life are hidden, and almost secretive? (e.g. *hidden underground fungus, page 9; some can only be seen under a microscope, page 13*)
- Point to the heading **Friendly fungus?** on page 6. Discuss the meaning of "friendly" in the context of fungus. (e.g. *helpful, supportive*) Challenge the children to look at pages 6 and 7 to:
  - decide whether fungus is "friendly" (*yes*)
  - find reasons for their answer. (e.g. *it helps life by being part of the cycle; it helps by eating up rotting things*)
- Look together at pages 22 and 23. Can the children remember something about these types of fungus? Encourage them to look back in the book if they're not sure.